ONE TO WON

DISCOVER THE *POWER* OF PARTNERSHIP

I0105884

MICAH AND TORRI GORDON

S.H.E. PUBLISHING, LLC

ONE TO WON
Copyright © 2021 by Micah & Torri Gordon.

Book Cover and Title Page design by Michelle Phillips of CHELLD3 3D Visualization and Design

For information, please contact:
W : www.shepublishingllc.com
E : info@shepublishingllc.com

ISBN :
978-1-953163-28-8 (paperback)
978-1-953163-30-1 (SheEdition)

Second Edition : October 2021

10 9 8 7 6 5 4 3 2 1

This book is dedicated to the power of
partnering with purpose.

CONTENTS

ONE TO WON

DISCOVER THE *POWER* OF PARTNERSHIP

MICAH AND TORRI GORDON

S.H.E. PUBLISHING, LLC

CHAPTER 1

The Power of
Individualized Growth

Growth: *the process of increasing in amount, value or importance.*

In any environment where culture shifts and economies are controlled through strong alliances, growth is a necessary adaptation. This is an adaptation you will have to make time and again, especially in long-term relationships.

Simply put: You have to grow WITH your partner. Personal and joint evolution is nonnegotiable, not identical advancement, but parallel.

You're a different person than them and may have a different capacity for expansion. Although growth is happening at the same time; it may be stretching you in another direction; and that is not a bad thing. You were raised differently and perhaps without comparable sensibilities. Therefore, the urgency to develop or redevelop in any particular area will still be different for you, as two individuals. Development with your partner may also be seasonal.

Some seasons of life don't allow for wiggle room, margin for error or mutual growth. Some situations are cut to fit and impossible to expand. However, in those instances, patience with yourself and your partner is important. When one of us decided to shift into a plant-based lifestyle, it provided a challenge to everyone in the house. Although we were not all on board initially, over time and with small daily changes, our family can now eat dinner together from one restaurant instead of placing three different take-out orders. Are we all vegan? No. Are we all dairy-free, not yet. Have we expanded our understanding of what eating healthy food and maintaining a healthy lifestyle means? Yes; and that is what it means to grow together. Do I still want a double bacon cheeseburger from time to time? Of course. Am I willing to forego it for a healthier option? Most of the time; and for me, that is progress at its finest.

How Can We Grow Separately Together?

Undoubtedly, people warned you that marriage is tough, but you probably thought that yours would be different, that it wouldn't be so hard. While marriage is an awesome part of life, it's not easy. If you're in the trenches of never-ending grocery lists, balancing your children's many needs and attempting to pay your mortgage while also maintaining some sort of sanity and romance, you're not alone.

Furthermore, even if you think you and your husband are pretty happy, it's normal for a relationship to gradually evolve. Not only because of the time you spend together (during which those little things that were once cute become rather irritating), but due to the fact that you're two individuals who are continuously changing and shifting, too. As Courtney Geter, a licensed marriage and family therapist explains, "A relationship is like a building or structure. Over time, buildings and structures experience wear and tear and need ongoing maintenance as well as intensive repair."

Nevertheless, before you schedule a therapy session, give your relationship a week. As many therapists and marriage experts agree, you can actually strengthen your bond, deepen your connection and reconnect by challenging yourselves for just 7 days.

Day 1: Stand in front of the mirror and Be honest with yourself.

A major part of this challenge is realizing that you have to put in the work to get results, and that means looking inward. Making a marriage stronger begins with the conscious decision to improve yourself. This is about what you are going to do, not what your spouse needs to do. Don't be afraid to stand in front of a mirror, look yourself in the eye and get real about what you want to change inside. Ask yourself what needs to shift for you to become stronger, better and happier as a person. Becoming the best version of yourself will strengthen your marriage more than anything else. If you need to, make a list.

Day 2: Choose one thing about yourself to Change that will make your partner happier.

By now, your partner knows who you are and what you aren't. They know what irritates you more than anything else, they know how you like your coffee and they can identify that look that means "don't talk to me right now." They also know what about you irritates them the most. Whatever those things are, give them your attention and figure out if there's something you can change, alter or stop doing. While you (obviously!) should never completely transform who you are, if there is something that you could be doing better or differently, why not just do it? If you know your spouse enjoys hugs more than anything in the world, make a conscious decision to hug him one to three times daily for the next week. If he's always complaining about caring for the pets, make the decision to take charge of daily dog walks and feedings for the next week.

In return, ask your husband to do the same. Maybe that's taking out the trash without being asked or bringing home flowers like he used to. The point is that you're erasing the small irritations that often cause a lot of fights. After a week, sit down and talk about "what those gestures meant to each of you."

Day 3: Greet your partner
Like you do your best friend.

When you see your bestie, do you roll your eyes in their general direction, make some sort of grumble of 'Hi' or instantly launch into a to-do list? Probably not. Sure, acting overly excited to greet the same guy that you see day in and day out seems like overkill, but according to couples therapist, Marni Feuerman, LCSW, LMFT, it's worth a shot. You may be surprised at how this relatively small, new and easy behavior steers your marriage in a different direction.

Day 4: Talk about how your last fight
Would have been covered on "Law & Order."

The difficult part about taking advice from friends or family is that they're biased. Your mom is probably always going to think you're the bee's knees, and your best friends might be brave enough to tell you when you're wrong, but maybe not. That's why Feuerman suggests trying the "emotional reappraisal" technique. When the house is quiet, sit down with your husband and talk about your latest disagreement.

Day 5: Look into
each other's Eyes for 5 to 10 minutes.

Therapists suggest doing this every single day, if it feels a little strange (warning: it probably will). During this time, heed a few ground rules: no touching, no talking and no distractions. That's right, nothing but loving eye-gazing. Looking into your partner's eyes builds emotional intimacy without the distractions of daily life. This activity may be uncomfortable at first, but keep with it and don't look away. After your allotted time, talk to your partner about what the activity felt like or the thoughts you had during the moment.

Day 6: Give more compliments—to Your partner and to yourself.

When was the last time that you truly, honestly complimented your spouse? Not just telling him that his butt looks great in those jeans or saying "good job" when he said his presentation went well, but for something genuine and specific? Perhaps more importantly, when was the last time you really gave yourself a pat on the back for all of your own amazing qualities? Not only are compliments easy to overlook, but their power is often understated.

We get so focused on trying to please others that we forget to acknowledge our own efforts and hard work. So every morning or night, look at yourself in the mirror and give yourself one compliment about your efforts in your relationship. Try to choose something different every day If you are a person who enjoys touch, give yourself a great big hug as well. These tricks are commonly used in therapy to help alleviate depression and anxiety, so why not try some self-therapy at home? While you're busy listing why you're awesome, do the same for

your husband. You might say, "I really love how supportive and encouraging you are with our son. He loves you and appreciates you so much, and so do I. You're a wonderful father."

Day 7: Start asking more questions.

If you want to feel those butterflies again, then you have to treat your partner like someone you just met. Part of the rush of an early relationship is discovering someone new. When was the last time you learned something sur-prising about your spouse, like what posters were in his room as a kid, how he got that scar above his elbow or where his own parents went on their honeymoon?

Feuerman encourages couples to ask questions daily—and not just about who is cooking dinner and who is picking up the dog from the groomer's—but real, get-to-know-you kind of questions. By treating your husband like a stranger, you get the chance to fall in love with him all over again.

Each and every one of us is unique; and we have our very own unique ways of expressing ourselves. Whether you are single or in a committed relationship, your individuality should not be ignored.

In my experience, the most important relationship is the one you have with yourself. If you cannot be true to yourself, all your relationships will inevitably suffer.

In addition, being in a romantic relationship takes work to keep it fun and exciting. There is nothing worse than feeling "stuck" in a relationship that has lost its spark.

In a relationship, there has to be room for both personalities to grow, individually as well as together. Because if not, you risk creating resentment towards each other, which has no place in a partnership.

Communication

Forgive me for pointing out the obvious here, but communication is key for any relationship to flourish. As obvious as it may seem, experience tells me that many couples have completely misunderstood the concept.

As I can attest, communication is more than just telling your partner what you need. I would argue that it is equally important, if not more important to actively listen for what they need.

The number of times I have had to lend a shoulder while friends complain that their partner "just isn't listening" is unfortunately shocking. However, if you ever find yourself in the same situation, I would urge you to stop and take a good hard look in the mirror and ask yourself: "Am I actively listening for my partner's needs?" Most often, I find that neither party shows a willingness to hear each other out.

Why not be the first person to allow your partner space to express their "side" and be completely honest in how they feel? This displays courage and helps to build trust. Most often, your partner will reciprocate and allow you the same.

At times, these types of honest conversations can be excruciatingly uncomfortable and scary. Trust me, I have had a few, but if we cannot be 100% honest with our partner, why are we even in a relationship in the first place?

Of course, to be honest with your partner, you first have to be honest with yourself. Again, forgive me for pointing out the obvious, but I know many individuals who are not living their authentic true selves.

If we are not living our true identity, we often unknowingly sabotage our partner's attempt to live theirs — thereby creating instability and mistrust. Yet, when you are living your true self, you inspire your partner to do the same and the relationship can flourish.

> Ask for Permission to Communicate
> Freely and Don't Make Assumptions.

When you feel you have something to express, don't put it on hold. Bottling up emotions is unhealthy and helps no-one. However, be courteous and respectful of your partner's time and feelings. Ask for permission to express yourself and wait for that permission to be granted.

A big mistake I used to make was to bottle up whatever was on my mind. I would go a couple of days snapping at my partner for no apparent reason. When everything finally burst out without warning, he would ask me why I'd waited so long to open up. I would make the excuse that I had too many thoughts swirling around my head to be able to make out what was going on and I needed time to find the words.

The truth is, often, I was embarrassed to admit that I had made assumptions about something he had said or done (or not done) and was afraid it meant the end of our relationship; a testament to my insecurities.

Waiting even a couple of days with something like that, sends your mind spiraling out of control. And in the end, when you finally have the conversation, you find yourself even more embarrassed that you had let your mind create scenarios that were completely out of proportion. We are not mind-readers. If you feel something is up, ask for permission to express yourself and ask questions. Do not make up the story.

Celebrate Each Other's Individuality

Most of us know once the excitement of falling in love subsides and things become "normal", the things we used to find adorable about our partners can start to annoy us.

When that happens, we often try to "change" their behaviors. We try to make them something they are not. If we succeed, we take away their individuality and personality, the very things we fell in love with in the first place.

In reality, most often, the things we want to change about someone else are either a reflection of some-thing we ought to change about ourselves or personal insecurities we need to resolve. This has become painfully obvious having spent years in self-reflection.

It is neither my responsibility nor my right to change any of my partner's attributes. Moreover, when it comes down to it, nor do I want to, there has to be room for each person to express themselves. We should encourage and celebrate our partners' individualities, not discourage them. It's what makes them unique and beautiful and we should thrive on that. We should be proud of that.

We wanted to share a few of the lessons we have learned on keeping a relationship growing, more often than not, the hard way. We've thrown things, we've yelled, we've wanted to quit and wallowed in the distance of anger, yet we've persevered and learned to grow a relationship that is as deep as it is wide.

Thoughts On Growing In a Relationship

You don't have to settle. You can grow your relationship and make it something that continually enhances your life. A good relationship is like anything you love; you must be committed to learning, to growing and always looking to improve. When you feel like you've settled, you need to act, or else that settling becomes a chasm of stagnation or worse.

Arguing is good. Many studies show that couples who argue have healthier relationships. It took a while to learn this in our relationship. For so long, I saw arguments as a failure, but the truth is that they are necessary components of a healthy relationship. To argue well, i.e. you can actually talk when the sparks are done flying, means you must respect each other and the relationship enough to fight for it.

Say you are sorry, and own it. When an argument goes bad, just walk away. Then when you can own your part in the debacle, return and say you are sorry. Expect nothing in return. This kind of unconditional response to adversity is a sure sign to your loved one that your relationship is more than skin deep.

Make time to talk about your relationship. Schedule time where you give each other an opportunity to talk about the relationship without judgement or animosity; and by "talk about your relationship", I mean treat your relationship like a third person. Are we talking enough, are their unresolved issues, etc.?

Remind yourself often of why you fell in love in the first place. Look at old pictures, tell old stories, remember those first magnetic embers of love. We aren't just who we are in this moment; we are a culmination of the past, the present and the future. Use the victories and lessons of the past as fuel for future growth.

Share small adventures. Our lives can get so busy we begin to forget about small pleasures. Go for walks, shopping together, coffee, whatever. When life has consumed us, even a short pleasure can seem like a walk on the beach.

Spend time totally focused on your partner. Massage them until your fingers cramp up, listen and don't talk, go with them on an errand they could do alone, write them a poem or love letter like you did when you were falling in love. Pray for them. Focusing on them will make the relationship stronger.

Schedule space for each other. You need space to grow. A suffocating relationship kills growth. We need freedom in the safety of a commitment. A strong relationship is one that is conscious of this space.

Keep track of your growth. Set goals for the relationship and keep track of them. Growing a relationship is like anything else of value; you need to plan, set goals, work and review.

A healthy relationship is two individuals working together. A healthy relationship is kind of like a trinity, two individuals create something deeper and better than themselves, yet they are still themselves. For a relationship to grow, you must also grow as an individual and not lose yourself. This can be really hard for mothers. They can get so caught up in their work, husband and children, that they don't know who they are anymore. Husbands, make sure you help her with that.

After 12 years of marriage, I can honestly say that the most exciting part of our relationship is what lies ahead. We made it through the incredibly hard process of learning to grow together and now the future seems filled with possibilities. Life is about living. Living is about growth. Any healthy relationship makes you better; it encourages you to grow, it is there for you when you stumble and falter.

A relationship is hard work, but if you commit yourself to planting the seeds of growth, you will see something beautiful you could never have imagined alone.

What To Do When Growth is Hard

There are two times when remembering to say "I love you" and committing to grow becomes especially important. The first is when things are going very badly between the two of you. The second is when things are going very badly for one or both of you with the rest of the world.

Let's start with troubled times between the two of you. Almost every relationship goes through difficult periods sooner or later. These are the times when you're displeased with almost everything your partner says or does, when everything goes wrong, when you can't understand your partner and he or she can't understand you; when whatever you do as you try to fix things seems only to make them worse; when you find yourself thinking that maybe your life would be better if the two of you separated, even though that's the last thing you really want. You begin wondering if you actually are still in love with your partner, although deep down you know you are.

Saying "I love you" doesn't come naturally during these times, but this is exactly when that statement is most needed. "I love you" is a healing phrase. It helps people get closer, countering the sense of isolation and distance from your partner that accompanies difficult periods. Saying "I love you" is a reminder that even though you don't like what your partner is doing, you still want him or her in your life. Now, of course just saying "I love you" won't solve any problems all by itself. Nor will it always turn things around right away (although sometimes it does indeed do just that). But it will help the two of you feel more hopeful about your relationship. Just make sure that "I love you" is never followed by the word "but," as in, "I love you, but you are wrong [stupid, ridiculous, thoughtless, mean . . .]."

Then there are the times when very discouraging events happen to one or both of you. A job layoff. A serious illness. A death in the family. Critical financial problems. Serious mental health problems such as anxiety or depression. A distant daughter. A troubled son. That's when you most need an ally in life, someone who will help you get through bad times. Here's what "I love you" means in these situations.

> *"You're not alone."*
> *"It's tough, but we'll get through it together."*
> *"I'll support you in every way I can."*
> *"We can do this." "Let me help you."*
> *"It's not the end of the world."*
> *"You can count on me."*

We hope that you and your partner are not at this stage in your relationship. However, if you are, the next exercise could be particularly important. If you're not, think back to the last time you and your partner were having big problems with each other or the world.

Some people think of love as a very private, very personal thing. Perhaps they just don't like displaying their emotions in public. Possibly they grew up in homes where their parents only displayed their affection behind closed doors. Maybe they even feel a little embarrassed or ashamed, as if it were silly or childish to be in love. The result, at any rate, is the same. These people seldom tell or show others they're in love. Their love remains a carefully guarded secret.

We think that's a mistake. Why? Because it is important that you let the world know that you're in love. There are actually several reasons this is so. First, telling others about your love may help that love grow stronger in your own heart. Saying "I love him [her]" often and to many people usually makes that love feel more real and powerful. Second, telling others about your love is a great way to honor your partner. It lets your partner know that you are proud of being in love with him or her. Third, love thrives when it is celebrated by the entire community. Anniversaries, for example, are times when a group gathers just to appreciate the ongoing love of two people for each other. Fourth, and perhaps the most compelling reason, is that it simply feels good to tell others about your great good fortune. You are in love. That's worth talking about.

No, you don't have to hire a pilot to write the name of your beloved in the sky. You don't have to write a love song and sing it in the rain. (Those aren't bad ideas either, but they are extra-special events.) We're talking about smaller, but more frequent conversations with your family, friends, coworkers and associates in which you mention your love. These are the kinds of conversations in which people normally talk about their partners. Sometimes they become complaint sessions: "My boyfriend is so stupid." "All my wife does is nag, nag, nag." "She's fat." "He's ugly." That's unfortunate. Bad-mouthing your partner only leads to feelings of anger, resentment and self-pity. On the other hand, telling others what you like about your partner solidifies your love and appreciation.

Prioritizing Your Growth

Let's face facts. Chances are your life is busy, busy, busy. You hustle from one task to another. You sleep less than you should. You eat fast food. You're constantly tired, but you have to keep going.

No wonder, then, that spending time with your partner gradually gets sacrificed. It's not usually a conscious choice so much as a slowly developing pattern. You go from taking hours each day alone with your partner to just scraping out a few minutes, and from doing things as a couple to only doing family activities. You talk less about important things. You joke around less with each other. Even your sex life erodes because you don't have time to feel very romantic. Worst of all, there seems to be no alternative. You feel stuck in this not-very-satisfying pattern because you have so much to do. You feel trapped.

However, there is a way out of this trap. It's called reprioritizing. **That means going from a list that probably looks like this:**

1- Job
2 - Kids
3- Chores
4- Other Responsibilities
5 – Partner

To a new list that goes:
1- Partner
2 - Everything else

Is that possible? Certainly! Is it easy? Actually, it's not as hard as you may think.

•   First, tell yourself that nothing, absolutely nothing, is more important to you than spending time alone with your partner. That must be your first choice because otherwise, everything else will squeeze it out.

•   Next, set a goal of spending at least thirty minutes a day alone with your partner. We're not talking about a pie-in-the-sky, wouldn't-that-be-nice dream, either. This has to be a real goal that you fully intend to keep.

• Figure out how you are going to make that happen. The best way is to develop a routine so you don't have to plan each day. For example, "We'll put the kids to bed fifteen minutes earlier every night and then spend a half hour just talking with each other before we go to bed."

• And then, make sure you follow through. That might mean telling the kids they cannot interrupt your evening half hour for anything short of a calamity; it might mean turning off the phone; it might mean leaving some work behind so you can get home on time.

• Finally, allow yourself no wiggle room. That means not accepting any excuses or explanations about why you can't take that time with your partner. Simply said, taking time with your partner must be so important to you that you make it happen. If you accept one excuse today ("I'm sorry, honey, but just tonight I have to stay longer at work"), then there will be another excuse tomorrow ("The car needs an oil change") and another the next day.

Here is a place for you to devise your game plan. Needless to say, you should make this plan with your partner since it involves both of you, but you and only you must take responsibility for carving out the time from your schedule to be with your partner.

Becoming Helpmates and Best Friends

We believe that two traditions of marriage coexist in America. On one hand, we want to work well with our partner: the old term "helpmeet" applies here, which we'll modify to "helpmate." In a well-functioning marriage, the partners are like two horses hitched to a heavy cart. Together, if they work harmoniously, they can pull that cart a long way. However, we also want our partner to be our best friend: someone we can talk with about anything, play with and generally enjoy. While the helpmate metaphor is two horses pulling a cart, the best friend model is more like two people holding hands walking side by side down the path of life.

Sometimes we meet couples in marriage counseling whose main problem is that one of them believes almost exclusively in the helpmate model while the other is totally tied to the best friend concept. The helpmate advocate thinks, "Life is hard. There's always a lot to get done. The house has to be painted. The kids need to be fed. I've got to have help with all this stuff or I'll fall apart." This person's chief complaint is that his or her partner doesn't do enough, doesn't carry a full load. The worst thing the helpmate person can call someone is "lazy". That shows how much he or she values working together.

Meanwhile, the best friend advocate thinks,"I didn't get into this relationship simply to work and work and work. I want romance, long talks, and closeness. I want my partner to tell me everything and I want to do the same." The best friend person's worst insult is that someone is "distant," which shows how much he or she values intimacy.

```
┌─────────────────────────────────┐
│   Show Your Desire to Grow by    │
│     Respecting Your Partner      │
└─────────────────────────────────┘
```

Understanding the word respect is absolutely critical if two people want to have a mutually loving relationship. That's because relationships without respect quickly become ugly and nasty, as each partner says things that are particularly hurtful to the other. Being in a relationship without respect is like sitting in a rowboat heading over Niagara Falls. Worse yet, it's like being the two people sitting in that boat who refuse to pick up their oars because they are too busy shouting insults at each other.

So what does it mean to respect someone? Perhaps the single most helpful definition of respect we've discovered is this one: "to show regard and consideration" (Random House Unabridged Dictionary, Second Edition). In addition to being generally polite and thoughtful, showing regard and consideration includes listening carefully to your partner and respecting his or her privacy.

The flip side of respect is called, naturally enough, disrespect. Disrespectful behavior is usually shaming, in that one person says or implies that there is something wrong with the other. Basically the shamer says that the other person is stupid, bad or worthless. The shamer is a judge who constantly convicts people of being no good, not good enough or unlovable; but what exactly does it mean to show regard and consideration to your partner?

Grow For as Long as It Takes

Timing is everything and growth takes time. You don't eat the fruit the day you plant the seed. It could take years for you to process those things that need pruning or those areas that require growth. A word of warning: All that time and all those years could be spent just arriving at the place of acknowledgement. Doing the hard work of self-examination can be all encompassing. Figuring out your triggers and the root of your dysfunction is just the tip of the iceberg. We haven't even begun to deal with the solution. This is where patience comes into play in a major way. Most likely, grace will have to be extended in both directions over time. The importance of allowing your partner to grow at their own speed is vital. The inner work required to accept those things about our character or personality that need attention is a reflection of growth. If growth is your goal, work and patience must become your best friends.

As you move throughout the world as a unit, there must be some evaluation and plan in place on a regular basis. Without that, you run the risk of stagnation, regression and loss altogether. Just like businesses have quarterly reviews, relationships should pause to process current viability. A plan for forward movement could be as simple as a weekly meeting:

Babe, how are we?
What could I be doing better?
What do you need from me?
How can I add value to our relationship?
What do I need to know?
What are your plans?

These can be hard questions to ask and answer at times, but being honest can only bring you all closer, once the dust settles. We have had some "knock-down, drag-out" evaluations. We have both left these conversations emotionally drained. We have both shared things about ourselves and feelings about each other that were miscommunicated or misinterpreted, and guess what?

That led to more conversations, but an essential part of growth is communication. Even when it's uncomfortable, talk it out. A part of being a mature adult is not retreating in the face of difficulty, but it does not happen like this. There are times when we are too emotional, too hurt, or don't have the words to communicate properly. And that's ok. For us, the key has been sitting together in the uncomfortable silences. Words can get in the way, but the conscious choice to love unconditionally and never stop evolving as a team must be made. Deciding that we are valuable to each other and that our relationship deserves to progress is a blessing.

The real jetpack for growth is assessing possible losses and gains to recalibrate together: togetherness. One-sided development will leave you deformed and disabled. What would your body look like if parts of it stopped developing altogether at different points, even though they are a pair? One big ear and one little one or one lung at 100 percent capacity and the other at 50? Hearing and breathing would prove difficult. The idea is to grow separately together. You may have different areas in which to improve, but there must be growth on both ends. The responsibility to do so falls equally. Whether you are side by side, or tandem, growth should be continuous. If it is simultaneous, that's even better. However, do not panic if that is not the case. Our next chapter gets you thinking together to figure it all out.

CHAPTER 2

The Power of Brainstorming

Brainstorming: *A group discussion to Produce ideas or solve problems.*

Communication is of utmost importance when trying to complete tasks. The ideas aren't always good, I'll be the first to admit, but the objective is to get them out on the table. Sharing the inner workings of one's mind can be scary. It takes thick skin, pliability and kindness on everybody's part.

Benefits of Communication in a Relationship

1. You Can Avoid Negative Misunderstandings.

How often do we misunderstand what the person really meant with a positive slant? We don't. For example, your partner says, "I'm tired of us fighting all the time." You may immediately assume he wants to end the relationship.

However, it is possible he means that he doesn't want to feel disconnected from you. He doesn't say that because he would perhaps feel too vulnerable and exposed. What if your response showed him you didn't really care about being disconnected? That would really suck for him.

So, by building a better understanding of what he often means, you will be avoiding the significant chance of misunderstanding what he is really trying to say. It may be that he may not know how to express what he truly wants to say.

2. Context Lessens Disconnections.
A disconnection (when someone feels upset) can be an occasional "blip" on a screen or feeling like you are constantly hitting an

emotional pothole. We are not always going to be in sync with what each other is really saying.

So, by increasing your general understanding of the other person and how they communicate, you are less likely to have the conversation go downhill. If it does, it will be much easier to reconnect, because you would be building a better "context" of one another once the person thinks about how they know the other person to really be and what their heart is really about.

3. You Can Determine
What They Are Really Saying.
Communication will feel easier as you build this new context of one another. You won't hesitate or shy away from asking those tough questions, like, "Why were you so upset with me?"

This is because each of you will be creating an understanding of your feelings towards the other person from the heart. So, when you two might be at "odds" over a particular subject, you will feel more emotionally safe in saying what you want to say because of the under-standing, or "context" that you are building.

4. You Avoid Arguments More Easily.
Due to the new "context", you'll both be building and you will "choose" to avoid the "potholes" rather than to argue. You will choose to understand the other person, rather than to stubbornly walk forward into a pothole you both will later regret.

As you both build a better "context" of each other, the positive benefits will become evident due to a more refined and accurate understanding between you two. You will each know and understand all of the good things you both really want in the relationship and how disappointed you feel after an argument.

5. You'll Be Willing to Give Each Other "Space."
Often during a fight, one partner wants to resolve the issue in order to feel better and to avoid worrying about the relationship.

The other person, however, often wants to get away from their mate in order to stop the argument because it is so uncomfortable. Sometimes, it is because one person is afraid that what they might say will really hurt the other person, and they don't want to do that.

At these times, when the "context" of the other person and the relationship status is more accurately understood, it becomes easier to give someone some time to cool off. It can feel less threatening to do so, because communication is often more positive and productive in general.

So, no one ends up feeling that the relationship is threatened by taking a time out to cool off, or to think about what they really want the other person to understand.

6. Trust Increases.
Once you have built context for one another, only one party at a time needs to practice the behaviors listed above, even when the other person currently not ready do this. By not responding in an equally negative and hurtful

manner, you will be building trust in the other person's eyes.

Eventually, the other person will see, through his or her new context of you, that you are not out to criticize, to control or "to get them."

Also, the other person will eventually begin to see that you no longer respond to them in a negative way; rather, you are responding in a productive way. You will be helping them to understand what you are really trying to say and that you are not out to make them feel bad about themselves.

It will also show that you are not trying to judge in a negative manner. This behavior is healthy in a relationship and absolutely builds trust over time. Of course, you need both parties to take their turn in this trust-building.

7. You Build Emotional Closeness and Intimacy.

So, reap the benefits! You've earned it! Now that you and your partner have learned how to understand each other more accurately, you both can begin to come forward more easily and more often. As he or she feels emotionally safer with you, he or she can come closer.

Men often have more difficulty with this context building. As the wife, if he doesn't know how to do this, show him by modeling the things talked about so far: not judging, controlling or criticizing him. Focus instead, on how you are feeling.

For example, Instead of saying in anger "You always do this!", you can say, "I really don't want us to be disconnected. I want us to feel closer to each other. What can I do to help you feel the same way?"

Someone has to be brave and take the risk in coming forward in a non-conflictual way. It might as well be you. Be the stronger person (but do not throw this in their face). Instead, model healthy communicationLet them see that you really want to feel closer to them emotionally and that you really value the relationship.

Recap: Seven Benefits to Communication In a Relationship:

1. You Can Avoid Negative Misunderstandings.
2. Context Lessens Disconnections.
3. You Can Determine What They Are Really Saying.
4. You Avoid Arguments More Easily.
5. You'll Be Willing to Give Each Other "Space."
6. Trust Increases.
7. You Build Emotional Closeness and Intimacy.

One of the best times to show that you love your partner is during a conflict. Why? Because most people fall away from secure attachment during fights with their partners and become more fearful, preoccupied or dismissive. They may look and sound angry, but they probably feel insecure, highly emotional and disconnected. In other words, it's just plain hard to feel loved during an argument. So that's exactly when people most need to get some reassurance. They need to hear right then and there that they are loved. Telling your partner about your love reassures him or her that your love is strong enough to weather any disagreement, however serious or long-lasting. It is one of the strongest statements of faith you can make.

So the first thing to remember is to say "I love you" to your partner even during conflict. However, there are other ways to show your partner your love during a disagreement. There are also some unloving things you will want to avoid doing.

Nine (9) Conversations That Every Couple Must Have

Having regular conversations about important topics can not only bring you and your spouse closer together right now, but can help you create a better plan for your future together. There is something powerful that happens when two people begin working towards the same goal! If it's been a while since the two of you have really talked, these 9 conversations every couple needs to have are a great place to start.

1. The Things That Make You Happy
It seems so simple, but in the busy hustle bustle of the day, we can lose sight of not only our own needs, but also our spouse's needs. Have a conversation about the things that truly make you happy and discover the same about your spouse.

Do you know the things that truly make him feel joy? Is it a fishing holiday with his buddies? Going to a concert to see his favorite band? (Do you know his favorite band?) Maybe he loves his morning run or a good cup of coffee. Maybe he loves watching the game with the kids.

Whatever it is that makes your spouse feel joy and satisfaction should become a priority for both of you. This isn't about only the things that you both enjoy, although those things are important, too. Learning what makes another person tick can really help you feel closer, even when you aren't together. It also helps you focus your priorities to be sure you're maximizing your joys as much as possible.

2. Money

Financial stress is the number one cause of divorce, and if you are sharing your life with someone, you MUST be able to discuss finances, debt and savings. Even if you keep your finances completely separate (which is nearly impossible, anyway), they still need to be discussed on a regular basis. In many states, spouses are on the hook for each other's debt, even if one passes away. You need to know where you stand.

There's nothing lonelier or more terrifying than hiding a secret, like debt, from your significant other. Finding out that your spouse is hiding a financial problem can be equally awful. Even if you're both great money managers, there's a high chance that you and your spouse handle money differently.

Discuss your weekly spending, your plans, previous debts and financial goals. Better yet, attend a Financial Peace University class together—make it a date night.

3. Your Parenting Styles

This is another "can't see the forest for the trees" conversation. Oftentimes, this conversation gets overlooked because we're just so busy being parents. However, continuously revisiting your parenting styles, objectives and thoughts on things like discipline, education and activities can be so important.

As our children get older, they often identify our parenting styles on their own, and at different times they may choose one parent over the other. It's easy to start to feel a little left out, but knowing that you're on the same page about the important parts helps solidify your bond as parents, together.

This conversation also helps immensely when your children attempt to play your styles off one another as they get older. (You know: "Dad will say yes, so ask him first, because mom will say no....") This is also something that'll save lots of headaches (and heaven forbid, nose piercings and curfew wars) when your children hit their teenage years.

4. The Things That Bother You
My husband and I fight. I'm willing to bet you and your spouse fight, too. It happens to the best of us. It doesn't mean we aren't in love or that our marriage is doomed. It just means we're two adults that live together—and it's bound to happen occasionally.

I have discovered that most of our fights come from little irritations that build up over time. We don't deal with them right away because they seem trite or trivial, or because we just don't have time. Nonetheless, when they happen again and again, that resentment builds up until it finally explodes.

That resentment can be poisonous to a relationship, and letting things build up until they reach the boiling point can cause irreparable harm. It is much better to deal with it proactively, before the anger sets in. If something is bothering you, bring it up gently. Tell your spouse how you're feeling in a non-accusatory way. Don't let it build. Simply say, "I feel bad about..." and explain.

Many times, little things that drive us crazy and drive wedges between us are not done on purpose. Chances are, your spouse may not even realize that a particular thing bothers you so much.

Saying you're sorry (and meaning it) is the other side of the coin. Sorry can be hard for some of us, because it means we're "admitting defeat." In reality, an apology can simply mean that you sincerely feel regret for hurting someone else. It may not change your conviction, but it can soften your approach.

5. Your Goals and Dreams

Family. A house. Financial stability. These things are pretty clear and are usually conversations you have early-on. As years go by and some of these things are locked down, be sure you still regularly revisit your long-term goals together.

Tackling a goal together—planning a vacation, plan- ting a garden or fixing up the guest room—can be a great way to spend time together and to remember that above all, you're always a team. You and that person you fell in love with are still in this one together.

Long-term goals can also be important. At what age does your spouse want to retire? Do you plan to stay in your home when your children are grown? Is there a life-long dream that still needs to be fulfilled? Keep these things in sight and work together to stay on the same page.

6. End of Life Care, Wishes and Plans

After avoiding it for a very long time, my husband and I finally took the time last year to meet with an attorney, create a will and settle our affairs. I'm not going to lie–it wasn't fun. We didn't relish the opportunity to think about our own mortality, or to imagine every worst case scenario, but we did it anyway, because we knew, after recently going through two deaths in our family, that it is important for the people who we will leave behind. Once that is done, I can't even tell you how much better it is to have that peace of mind!

Death is something none of us want to think about, especially not when we're with our loved one—but it's a necessity. Life can be uncertain. Perfectly healthy people have terrible accidents. We owe it to our children and our spouses to have this conversation.

If one of you is incapacitated, what are your wishes for care? What are your burial wishes? Who would take care of your children and your finances in the event that both of you were killed? It may seem morbid, but this conversation will save others from having to make decisions based on speculation at a time of bereavement.

Every couple should also have a will and life insurance. There are plenty of ways to set up a will online, or a local attorney will be able to take care of everything for around $500-$1000, depending on how complicated you need it to be. Talk to your financial manager or your 401(k) investment firm about setting up life insurance, your beneficiaries and what your other financial needs might be in case of unforeseen circumstances. This can be one of the most difficult conversations to have, but in the long term it will give you both peace of mind, and protection.

7. Things That Make You Blush

Your spouse should be your confidant. After all, you've surely shared plenty of intimate, private and vulnerable moments together. Now I'm not saying you have to share every glaring detail with each other at all times, or that you can't still enjoy your privacy, but allow yourself to share things that might make you feel a little embarrassed.

These topics can run the gamut from intimate needs and racy ideas to health concerns or even mortifying moments you just have to get off your chest. Intimacy is about sharing things that can be hard to say, but sharing them can be freeing and solidify the closeness you share. Think of something you've never told anyone and share it with your spouse. Chances are, you'll learn something new about them as well.

8. The Reasons You Love Each Other

Compared to finances and catastrophe, "Why do you love me?" can seem like a trite question—but I promise, it's no less vital to the health of your marriage. Ladies, look at your spouse and think of that guy that gave you butterflies in your stomach when he looked at you. Think of all the ways he's a great father and how you grin every time you see him take your daughter's little hand.

Look at his eyes and remember how many times you've gazed into them and felt love. How many times have you caught his eye in a crowded room and felt relieved because you were trying to get his attention? Look at his hands and think of how you'll always love them, even when they're old with thin skin and blue veins, and how you'll still long to hold that hand for comfort. Guys, do this as well for your wife!

9. Your Faith
Our relationship with God strengthens our marriages and helps give us guidance when facing life's challenges. I've seen many relationships falter because two people didn't share the same beliefs—or more often, because they chose not to discuss how their faith and relationship with God has changed over time. I've also seen many marriages strengthened because the couple took the time to regularly discuss their faith, and of course, because they've leaned on each other through tough times when their mutual faith was shaken.

Marriage can be hard, there's no doubt about that. However, it is much, much harder when communication is not a part of the equation. Regular conversations about the things that matter most will make all the difference, and if any of these things are topics you and your spouse haven't discussed lately, make a date and make it a priority–I promise you won't regret it!

Recap: Nine (9) Conversations Every Couple Needs to Have:

1. The Things That Make You Happy
2. Money
3. Your Parenting Styles
4. The Things That Bother You
5. Your Goals and Dreams
6. End of Life Care, Wishes and Plans
7. Things That Make You Blush
8. The Reasons You Love Each Other
9. Your Faith

Two Heads Are (Usually) Better Than One

When it comes to formulating, planning and strategizing, having a partner who is an open channel is invaluable. In my own marriage for example, we generally work in tandem this way during the beginning stages of a project to get the ball rolling and then we delegate and make progress on our own. While Micah is the quarterback, I often find myself in the end zone waiting on a Hail Mary. He's the prompt guy, the spark. I am usually able to take his initial idea or concept and flesh out the details to bring it full circle.

It took us a few bumps in the road, but we quickly figured out that sharing the load can make any project less taxing. Although, in order to really do that, you have to identify your strengths and weaknesses. Distinguishing these is really the only way to tackle a project head on with any degree of certainty. This means you have to know yourself and your partner; and that level of knowing requires honesty and communication. If you are forgetful and lack business acumen, it is ok to relinquish control of your family business affairs to your partner who may have been balancing a checkbook since fifth grade. If you are lucky, you may have found yourself partnered with someone whose skillset fills in the blanks in yours, and vice versa.

When you are experts in different areas, you can offer balance and be complementary. When there is diversity in approach, you can come at projects from a new angle. It can, however, prove difficult if you both happen to be an expert at the same thing.

As different as we are, we share the joy of being writers. Both Micah and I have a love for writing, and it's not just a passion play; we are actually pretty good at it. Our War Room is adequately dressed and appropriately named. This is a dedicated space in our home where we have written songs, angry customer service letters, full albums, copy, courses, curriculums and now books. We have had shouting matches and shed tears over lyric changes and uncleared samples on interludes. We have gone to the mat for the ideas we believe in. The environment has grown to be one that is honest and tempered with love. That, sometimes, makes for hard critiques, clenched jaws and resolving to agree to disagree sometimes. That happens because we feel a sense of entitlement since our skill level is comparable. Both of our voices deserve to be heard and there's a 100% chance at least one of us is right!

When we were working on my second album, Stained Glass Window, I was in my bag. I was confident and was the only one of us who had made a record at that point. In our war room, I never hesitated to remind my partner of that. It proved to be an exercise in futility because, experienced or not, Micah was a brilliant lyricist. We would go back and forth over lines, squabbling over the minutia until one day, we'd both had enough. I had forgotten the main part: although I was the "artist", it was a collaborative effort. We both would take cues from outside before listening to each other. There was no way the tension would lift if we didn't decide to meet in the middle. Right before we both gave up, I got off my high horse and warmed to the idea that I might not be the best writer in my house and Micah learned to express himself in ways that helped me understand where he was coming from. We still did not always agree, but there was a dance. A back and forth. An exchange was occurring.

Without a doubt, that's what BRAINSTORMING is. We were able to put ourselves in an open headspace and heart space. It reminded us that some things you will have to know, others you will have to feel. When we were firing on all cylinders, it was palpable. We are grateful for those watershed moments that really cemented our bond and our brand of collaboration. For you, it may not be song lyrics, it might be the financial future of your family, religion or lemon pound cake recipes. Relationships require that tug of war to build resistance elsewhere.

CHAPTER 3

The Power of Quality Time

Quality Time: *time spent in giving another person one's undivided attention in order to strengthen a relationship.*

I f I just lay here, would you lie with me and just forget the world? Song lyrics often shape our lives, not just provide the soundtrack. This song was a staple the first couple years of our marriage. I remember thinking, *what can we do that will allow us to leave everything and everyone behind and just be together? Just me and you? Us.* You know that feeling when you get into a good groove with your partner? The energy is just right. Random compliments, heartfelt encouragement, foot rubs while watching Hulu. The hope that those moments and that life could be the norm and not the one-off excited every fiber of our beings. I grew up watching the Cosby show and I fantasized about sitting in the bed on a Sunday morning reading the paper and laughing with my husband or watching nature documen- taries and creating family memories like Cliff and Claire. Little did I know, way across town, there was a young man hoping for the same thing. We have been so blessed to fit together comfortably in any cuddle position and have argued over couch purchases based on its ability to support proper spoonage. It was a struggle to figure it out. Work and some semblance of an outside life is what was making it impossible for us to just BE.

Creating A Work/Life Balance

If a man doesn't work, he doesn't eat. That goes for men who are in love too. As idealistic twenty-somethings, we were serious about not spending the rest of our lives beholden to an employer. So we took an inventory and discovered that unfortunately we could not make it beyond the six-month mark trying to live solely off our savings. We also had no profitable skills to start our own money generating endeavor. Most of the things we found ourselves involved in were extremely fulfilling, but did not bring in the bank we needed to survive. We performed for small groups of people locally doing original music and made cupcakes. Unfortunately, that wasn't enough to cover our meager bills or other stuff like food, healthcare and air! It did, however, cement the reality that we could work together professsionally, which made us feel invincible as a team. Grinding it out in those early days, couponing, saving and sacrificing yielded more than financial stability taught us that we could do it; and by it, I mean anything. Micah has this incorrigible drive that is only matched by his consistency. I was super resourceful and was discovering alternative creative paths that generated needed income. It still was not enough to buy the one thing we wanted more than anything: TIME, and that's the real play. If you are amassing wealth to buy things, you've got it all mixed up. The ultimate goal should be, in the words of the great Maxine Waters, to "reclaim your time".

That 40-to-60-hour work week was killing us, physically and relationally. We work better together and require a high level of connectivity. That is almost impossible to believe given our personal histories. As the youngest child of a single mother, Micah spent a large portion of his childhood feeling like an only child, because of the age differences between him and his older siblings. Still a loner, even by the time I met him in our twenties, he was just fine by himself, until I came along. I am the queen of autonomy. I enjoyed being an occasional extrovert professionally but once the cameras stopped rolling, I was at peace alone.

When we connected, something changed for both of us. We found a home in each other. That happened because we were able to have the time to build that connection. We spent a solid year together in a one-bedroom condo.

Nowhere to run to. Nowhere to hide. We faced so many issues head on during that period of our lives because we had no choice. They tell you that you should never go to bed mad at your spouse, but what they don't say is never start an argument at 10:30 pm. Quality time added value to us as individuals and as a team.

Eventually, corporate America came calling again for Micah and my work in ministry was being brought to the forefront. This allowed for financial growth, but little to no "us time", that thing that was "our thing". We'd prided ourselves on our ability to escape into each other and not much else, but in the real world, sometimes you get two weeks of vacation per year and that's all. No three-day weekends away on a whim; no time was left for all-night sessions filled with life-changing conversations.

We had been spoiled by the freedom to live and be together. We had grown accustomed to phones on "do not disturb" and metered out interactive time with everyone else. How would we survive? Intentionally, that's how. We were deliberate about creating a space for just us, even if it was a four-hour block on Sunday nights. It represented what we both needed so desperately: connection to each other.

Finding the balance between work and relationships isn't easy, but it's a necessary evil. What do you do when there aren't enough hours in the day? Plan properly.

> If You Fail to Plan, You Plan to Fail.

It seems like married life has brought so many adages to reality. Having a plan was the only way we could pull it off. So we got out the notes app on our phones and two composition notebooks. We tried our best to list our goals and find a way to get there together.

Even this book was years in the making. It is born from a belief that if you know something helpful, you should share that knowledge. We stand on the shoulders of those who have modeled for us how to coexist peacefully and prosper.

It is vital to be able to block out distraction, other people's ideologies and agendas to focus on your goals as a couple. The easiest way to do it is together.

> ## Carving Out Quality Time

1. Text Each other during the day

I will be the first to tell you that my husband is way better at doing this than I am. I will usually get a text sometime mid-morning telling me that he loves me and is thinking about me. Sometimes it just says "I love you and hope you are having a good day." When you send your spouse a sweet text, using their name or a pet name that you always call them makes it more meaningful and is just a little tip to help make the message more personal.

My husband and I seem to live in vastly different worlds during the day and it is easy to get to feeling like I am all alone and disconnected from him. The texts that he sends me during the day are a huge 'pick me up'. It tells me that he loves me, is thinking of me and cares about me and my day. If I am having a bad morning or even if nothing is happening, seeing a text from him just gives me a warm fuzzy feeling and that little extra "push" that makes it easier to get through the day. This is a great way to invest some quality time when there is not much time to be had. It lets you know that your spouse is thinking of you, even if they are not there.

2. Make a Lunch Call

This is never a very long call. I think most of our lunch calls are between 3-5 minutes, but oh how I look forward to them! I love hearing his voice mid-day and hearing how he is doing and how his day is going. This is just another way that we stay connected during the day and help to make our "worlds" a little closer. Again, this one is quality time, even if it is only 3-5 minutes. It makes the day go by so much faster!

3. Eat Dinner as a Family

I know that many families are busy running everywhere, but I love eating supper as a family. Maybe I'm old-fashioned like that, but for us, it gives us a sense of togetherness and time to connect with one another and talk. Marriage should be a 3-fold cord: God, husband and wife. When children are added, they further strengthen the bond. I think it is important to make time for a meal together as a family as often as you can. It may be grabbing a burger at the local fast food joint and eating around the table there, but the important thing is the conversation that naturally bubbles up around the meal, and that is something that you are doing together as a family. It gives a sense of "we're all in this together," which is one of the major benefits to quality time.

4. Cuddling/Physical Contact

Cuddling is a simple way to connect with your spouse. It lets your spouse know that you are there, you love them and both of you are in this crazy thing called life together. There is something soothing and connecting about physical contact with another person and it is deeper with your spouse than with anyone else. Even when I am exhausted, I can usually rely on this one for quality time. There is something very relaxing about falling asleep on my husband's shoulder.

5. Spend time together and communicate

The heading above says "communicate" and not just talk. Communication includes talking, but it goes much deeper, because it implies a mutual understanding. Some of the best times that my husband and I have had, occurred when we turned off all electronics and sat on the couch. We naturally start talking and listening to one another. It started with me. I told him all that was on my mind and the things that were happening. With his quiet listening and encouraging comments, I poured out all my worries and concerns; and he listened. I don't mean that he was just quiet and a million miles away. He was there, he was quiet, but he was engaged and listening to understand, not to reply or to solve my problems.

Sometimes, instead of me, it is his turn. Other times we sit and dream about what we would like to do or plan a vacation (fantasy or real) that we would like to take. Sometimes we reminisce or talk about our family. We just let the conversations flow naturally. These are the times that we really connect and I feel like the time we have spent together are some of the best quality times we have. The conversations help to bring us closer, and we fall in love with each other all over again.

6. Run Errands Together

I married my husband for many reasons, one of which is because he is my best friend. There is no other person that I would rather hang out with. We may be going to Target to have the time of our lives or Walmart to pick up a few things that we need. It doesn't matter to me where we are going or what we are doing, as long as I'm with him. Occasionally, we get the chance to run short errands together without

the kids and we refer to them as "mini-dates."
This one may not feel as much like quality time
as some of the others, but it is most definitely a
good time investment.

7. Work on a Project Together

Life is not all fun and games (as I'm sure you
know all too well). Sometimes spending quality
time together can be working on a project
together. My husband and I have done several
projects together. Most of them are related to
fixing something around the house. I will make
a confession here: I HATE construction and
fixing things! However, sometimes he would
need an extra hand, and I was the only one
available. When we were younger, I was pretty
cranky about it, ut as our marriage matured
over time, I started to value it as time together.
Bonus: We fixed the things that needed fixing!

8. Try to Fulfill a Need

Whether it's big or small, paying attention to
and communicating about your needs is of
utmost importance in any successful relationship. It boils down to observant love. If

they are complaining about being stressed and having back pain, set up a massage therapy appointment. It seems simple enough, but we fumble opportunities to serve and cater to our spouse this way all the time. If you see a need, fulfil it and watch your spouse change their behavior. Look to see if your spouse has a need that is not being met, and try to find a way to fulfill that need. It will be one of the most meaningful things that you can do for them.

9. At Home Date

Regular date nights out are wonderful and I am all for them! We enjoy them immensely when we can. However, we do not always have the time for them. Sometimes we find all our weekends obligated with other activities. Sometimes a babysitter is not available. However, we can usually find the time for a date night.

Our Favorite At-Home Date Ideas for Quality Time. We usually try to do this after the kids are in bed and what we do varies. We have laid outside on a blanket in the yard and watched for shooting stars. Other times, it's snuggling up on the couch for a movie that is not animated, you know, the ones with real live people in them?! Personally, I think our favorite thing to do is for my husband to pick up some sushi rolls from our favorite restaurant and have a late supper together after the kids go to bed.

We have dressed this idea up and down depending on how tired we are. Usually, I have no make-up on, in a sweatshirt, jeans and my hair in a pony-tail, as we start eating off paper plates in the kitchen.

Whatever you decide to do, make it fun and come up with something that fits your personalities and interests.

10. Vacation as a Family

Even as a child, I loved family vacations. They were such good "together" quality time moments, which made memories together that I still cherish. Vacationing together helped with the communication between myself and my husband as well. He is a planner and I am spontaneous. Do you see a problem here? Had we not vacationed together, we might not have addressed that issue. We had to learn some give and take. That strengthened our relationship and I would not give anything for the memories we have made together while on family vacations.

Recap: Ten (10) Ways to Carve Out Quality Time:

1. Text Each other during the day
2. Make a Lunch Call
3. Eat Dinner as a Family
4. Cuddling/Physical Contact
5. Spend time together and communicate
6. Run Errands Together
7. Work on a Project Together
8. Try to Fulfill a Need
9. At Home Date
10. Vacation as a Family

Make Time for Affection

Sixty years of research in the area of parent-child attachment validates one theme: human beings are internally hardwired to receive nurturance from other human beings. Actually, we're programmed to demand nurturance, as anyone who's ever tried to ignore a hungry infant for a few minutes can attest. Indeed, we begin life anything but helpless. Infants are born with a "Take care of me—now!" signal system that generally works quite effectively. Women (and we think some men, too) are biologically programmed to respond to an infant's needs. Otherwise, what good would it do for the infant to cry?

Gradually, infants respond to the parent answering their cry, not just by quitting crying but with a smile. They recognize their parents' faces. A special bond develops that changes "I'm any baby being taken care of by any mother" into "I'm a unique child being taken care of by my one and only one mommy." That's how "Feed me" evolves into "Love me." From a child's point of view, then, you can't separate being loved from being nurtured. To a child, it's completely normal, natural and necessary to take in another's love.

Life gets a little more complex by the time we reach adulthood. The nurturing in adult romantic relationships usually is two-directional. Each partner gives and receives nurturance from the other. (Not always in equal amounts, though. One common complaint we hear in marriage counseling is that one person thinks he or she gives way more than 50 percent to the other. More often than not, in American society, it is the woman who feels overburdened and undernurtured.) In addition, adults have a very wide range of wants and needs. It's no longer just "Feed me" but "Feed me and hold me and make love to me and spend time with me and talk with me and listen to me and tell me you love me." However, our main point is almost the same as before: just as with children, it's natural, normal and necessary for adults to take in their partner's love.

Somewhere along the path of life, however, some people may have lost touch with this simple truth. If that has happened to you, then you shy away from taking in nurturing and love. In particular, you often ignore, decline or reject your partner's attempts to take care of you. Perhaps you grew up in a home where you didn't observe much love-giving or love- taking, so it doesn't seem right to want that now. Maybe you were told that people should only give and never receive. Whatever the reasons, today you realize that you don't take in a lot of the love that your partner offers you. Consciously or subconsciously, you commonly deliver a "No, thanks, dear" message to your partner. "No, thanks; I don't want your caring. No, thanks; I don't need your tenderness. No, thanks; I won't take your comfort. No, thanks; I can't take your love."

Nobody can make you accept love, care and kindness. You can block it forever, but why would you want to? Declining to take in your partner's love makes about as much sense as refusing to eat at a banquet or rejecting a warm blanket on the coldest day of the year. All that goodness is right there. All you have to do is receive it.

CHAPTER 4

The Power of Teamwork

Teamwork:
*the combined action of a group of people,
especially when effective and efficient.*

Teamwork Makes the Dream Work. If you want to live a fairytale life, get ready for some company. There are so many moving pieces to our everyday existence, I couldn't imagine doing any of it alone. Joining forces works so well when done properly.

Identifying Roles Within the Team
Someone has to be the coach, someone has to be the star player, someone has to be one who

grinds it out of the blocks every night. Who-ever you are on the team, it becomes more important to play your role each game. Crea-ting a playbook or plan of action is also one of the tools we have utilized throughout the years to stay on track and keep our goals within sight.

Team sports are interesting, because of the team dynamic and load sharing that you do not have in individual sports. It is the same reason why boy bands from the 90s and 2000s out-sold the majority of solo artists. Teams/groups also fare better because they offer a wider reach. I may not be a Justin Timberlake fan, but in a group context, I can still buy his album because of my fascination with Joey Fatone. We see it in families as well. That aunt and uncle you love so dearly are likely winning because of the strengths they have together. She remembers the birthdays; he handles the cookouts. There is much to gain from not being solely responsible for the "W". Even the greatest of all time, Michael Jordan never won a championship without Scottie Pippen. Sure, he was undoubtedly able to play and extremely gifted, but was not able to actually win until partnered with someone who offered balance and support.

Compartmentalization is key when it comes to navigating business and personal relationships. The ability to put things in their proper place is integral to peace. We all have things we excel at; regardless of what you as your spouse have in common, there are key differences to your skillsets that make partnering the most viable option. If we were all the same, how would the world benefit? Our usefulness is tied to our uniqueness. In relationships, we can bounce off each other and make it happen by teaming up.

Importance Of Teamwork In Relationships

The importance of collaboration in the workplace has become extremely emphasized in most organizations. However, do you apply those same concepts to your relationships?

Most people do not consider teamwork in the same way when they enter into a long-term relationship or marriage. However, that same concept of collaboration is what makes your relationships strong and able to withstand significant life changes and obstacles.

Brings You Closer Together

Whether you are looking at your relationships with your friends, your boyfriend/girlfriend or your spouse, there is no doubt that teamwork brings people closer together. When you work together as a team to tackle problems or daily life activities, it helps you to form a bond with those closest to you. This is a bond that simply cannot be created when two people are constantly working apart.

Teamwork Lightens The Load

Teamwork lightens the load for everyone involved. When you work together as a team, no one bears the responsibility of handling everything on their own. It is vital to make sure that as parents, you don't get burned out or overwhelmed with the stress of daily life, especially in relationships where you are caring for multiple children.

Teamwork Improves Relationships

As humans, we tend to do things for people we like or love. However, we also tend to love or like the people who do nice things for us, even more. This is known as the Benjamin Franklin effect. The importance of teamwork in relationships is that it allows everyone involved to help each other. The more you help each other, the stronger your bond will become.

With Teamwork, Compromise Becomes Possible

When each person in a relationship is working alone, reaching a mutual agreement becomes difficult. Each person has their own ideas of how things should be, and they are not likely to mesh. However, when you work together as a team, compromise becomes more likely. You can work together to come up with ideas and solutions that you both gave input on and can live with.

Teamwork Brings Twice As Many Ideas

Working alone, you may have some ideas for solving problems that will ultimately work. But is there a better idea? When you work together with your partner as a team, you come up with at least twice as many ideas together as you would separately. The more ideas you have, the more likely you are to come up with viable solutions.

Teamwork Builds Successful Relationships

A successful team puts the needs of the team and the members above themselves, while still making sure that they can contribute effectively to the organization through self-care. The same is true of relationships. When you are in a relationship, you need to be able to put your significant other above yourself while you take care of yourself and do what you need to do for you. Being part of a team involves sacrifice, self-lessness and perseverance.

Teamwork Opens The Lines Of Communication

Teamwork opens up the lines of communication in a way that few other things can. When working together as a team, you have to be able to communicate effectively with one another to solve problems, come up with ideas and get the job done. This requires not only being able to tell your partner what you want them to know, but also really improving your listening skills. The more you practice being a team, the easier the communication will become.

Notice The Times
When Your Partner is Caring And Considerate

They're right there, waiting for you to observe. The coffee that's ready for you when you wake up. That call just to say hello while you are at work. A Netflix movie that is exactly the type you like most. Kind words. A playful touch on your arm. The extra time with the kids so you can finish your nap. Something special said or done during lovemaking that makes you feel really good. A small gift given for no reason. Each of these things is your partner's way of saying "I think about you a lot, I want you to be happy and I love you."

However, what if you don't notice these gifts? Perhaps you've never paid attention to such acts of kindness and consideration, or maybe lately, you're too busy thinking about something else. By not noticing, you fail to acknowledge them or to thank your partner. That's no big deal when it happens once in a while, but eventually you will pay a heavy price for your inattention. Unrewarded, your partner will begin cutting back on those nice words and deeds.

How To Avoid Only Looking For The Bad Stuff

We understand that most people become defensive for a reason. Perhaps your partner has said some really mean things to you that are hard to forget. Maybe you have felt set up because what started out as a compliment turned into a criticism ("Honey, thanks for doing the laundry, but you forgot to take the clothes out of the dryer and now they're all wrinkled. You never do anything right, do you?"). So you've become negative about the entire relationship. Okay, that's understandable, but now you have a choice. Will you continue to be defensive, to assume the worst about your partner, or will you give him or her the benefit of the doubt and quit being so defensive? If you want to take the second option, do these things:

- Keep looking for the good things your partner does.
- Consciously remind yourself not to be defensive.
- If you do notice that you are becoming defensive, take a deep breath or two and let that defensiveness float out of your system.
- Tell yourself this: "I know my partner is on my side. He (or she) is not the enemy so I shouldn't treat him (or her) that way."
- Make a list of everything you think, say and do when you become defensive. Then make a new list of things that you can think, say and do to quit being defensive. For instance, if you fold your arms tightly around your body when you get

defensive, let your arms drop to your sides instead.

Give Your Teammate the Ball

There are many people who don't tell their partners what they want because they think it would mean more if their partner figured it out without help. Their idea is that they would feel more loved if their partners knew them well enough to read their minds or could intuitively sense what they wanted or needed. These people say, "If you loved me," "you would know that . . ." etc. Most of the time that's not true. Love does not automatically lead to understanding. Your partner can love you deeply and still not know about something you really want or need. Good partners don't necessarily think alike and certainly cannot be expected to be mind readers.

There is a general principle here that applies to many aspects of a relationship: don't create tests for your partner to see if he or she really loves you. When you do so, only two things can happen: (1) your partner will fail the test and you'll feel unloved or (2) your partner will pass the test, so you'll create another until eventually he or she will fail the test and you'll feel unloved. Testing belongs in schools, not relationships.

On the other hand, you can and should create opportunities for your partner to show caring and be loving. But there is a big difference between giving your partner a test and giving him or her an opportunity. You can't fail opportunities. True, your partner might miss some opportunities to be loving that you offer. Perhaps he could have brought you flowers for your birthday but forgot. Perhaps she could have showed a little more appreciation for the hard work you just did around the house. You'll probably feel a little disappointed when that happens, but you'll still feel loved. Besides, there will be more opportunities for your partner to show they care down the line. Let's return to the matter of telling your partner what you want. If there is something important you want from your partner, you need to tell him or her about it. Telling your partner offers him or her an opportunity to respond. Not saying anything, though, creates one of those "If you love me, you . . ." tests that are a setup for resentment. So go ahead and mention that you want more alone time, more together time or more cuddling time or more shared activities or whatever else really matters to you. Here is a place for you to write down any of your "If you love me, you . . ." tests.

Be sure to think about this carefully as you start writing. Sometimes these love tests are partly subconscious. You have to be really honest with yourself so you can bring half-conscious material into full awareness. One way to identify these hidden tests is to remember times you wanted something badly from your partner but you didn't say anything. Or perhaps you hinted so vaguely that you created a guessing game or a puzzle that your partner couldn't solve. Perhaps you asked for something totally unreasonable that guaranteed your partner's failure, or maybe you expected and even wanted your partner to fail so you could feel miserable. Make sure you write down any of these love test games that you are still playing.

Perhaps you've reached a growing edge in your religious or spiritual life. The old explanations of the meaning of life don't feel quite right anymore. Dissatisfied with what's inside your comfort zone, you may decide to try out a couple of new churches in your denomination. If that doesn't work, you may have to take another step, perhaps exploring another denomination or a more individualized spirituality. You're not planning to convert to an entirely new religion, though. That would be way past your growing edge and into the complete unknown.

All romantic relationships go through ups and downs and they all take work, commitment and a willingness to adapt and change with your partner. Whether your relationship is just starting out or you've been together for years, there are steps you can take to build a healthy relationship. Even if you've experienced a lot of failed relationships in the past or struggled before to rekindle the fires of romance in your current relationship, you can learn to stay connected, find fulfillment and enjoy lasting happiness.

CHAPTER 5

The Power of Calculated Risks

Calculated Risk: *a chance taken after careful estimation of the probable outcome.*

A trust fall is a team-building exercise in which a person deliberately allows themselves to fall, trusting the members of a group or one spotter to catch them. There are many less-than-desirable elements of the trust fall. The primary variant being, the person falling has to be able to rely on the person who's supposed to catch them. The same is true of personal and business relationships. As a vendor, you must be able to meet the demands of the buyer and suppliers. As a parttner, you must be able to expect and deliver on promises made as well.

There will be difficulties beyond belief, but reliance on another person is one of the most beautiful parts of a real relationship. Sometimes, it is not until you're able to prove your trustworthiness that a partner is able to go all in with you.

There are lots of risks that you take in life, from big, life-changing risks to smaller, day-to-day gambles. Sometimes you have to sort of go at it alone on the risk-taking front, but when you're sharing your life with a partner or family, the risks you choose to take or stay far away from can affect everyone, not just you. So how can you make sure that the risks you're taking are not only smart and made mindfully, but are also beneficial for you and your partner? There are some calculated risks you and your partner can take together to strengthen your relationship, bring the two of you closer together and inject a little energy into your relationship as well.

"When you take a risk, you are letting your partner know that you trust them and that they are 'your person'; you are turning towards them not away from them (this an aspect of relationships that research shows is an indicator of strength and longevity), you are building intimacy through shared unique experience, you are building your own self-esteem by taking a risk, and high self-esteem is directly correlated to better partnership," Tracy K. Ross, LCSW, a couples therapist and relationship expert, tells Romper in an email exchange. Risks have the power to make things better, even if it doesn't always seem likely that they will. While taking a risk might not be able to perform any kind of miracle or completely save a relationship, trusting each other enough to take risks together certainly can make it stronger.

> ## Risks Worth Taking

1. Sharing Your
Fantasies or Mixing Things Up a Bit
Wendy Newman, a relationship expert and the auth- or of 121 First Dates, says that mixing things up and having sex somewhere unex-pected or unusual for you is one sort of risk that you can take together. Additionally, talk-ing about fantasies or likes and dislikes can feel like you're taking a chance, even though it's relatively low-risk. Newman says that

taking risks like these can bring some of that "playfulness" back into your sex life and into your relationship.

2. Moving

Moving might not seem like a risk, but if you're making the decision to move away from friends, family or a city that's familiar, it can feel a little daunting. Heidi McBain, a licensed professional counsellor, says that moving can be a risk that the two of you take together that could strengthen your relationship. "If they are in it together, it can bring them closer because they having to problem solve and make big decisions together," McBain says. You'll likely have to rely on each other a lot to get settled in your new home and facing those challenges together can make your relationship stronger.

3. Going to Couples Therapy

For some couples, going to couple's therapy can certainly feel a little risky. "Working through some of your problems as a couple can be a very worthwhile Endeavor," says Jonathan Bennett, a certified counsellor, life coach and dating and relationship coach. "Even attending a few sessions with a relationship counsellor or coach could provide insights you'd never have considered. However, seeing a therapist involves admitting that your relationship isn't perfect, a bold move many couples fear making." Plus, therapy often requires you to be vulnerable and that can always feel like you're taking a bit of a chance.

4. Starting A Family
Deciding to start a family can also be a calculated risk. It's likely that you'll have some concerns, fears or issues to work through, but you can face them together, as long as you're open and honest with each other about what those things might be (which itself can feel like another little risk). "Communication is key during any life change that the couple is going through because things will come up that they did not anticipate, and these are the things they are going to have to figure out as a couple, together," McBain says.

5. Committing
Taking the leap and committing to your partner is always a tiny bit risky because, of course, you don't want to get hurt—and you probably don't want to hurt them either. According to Dr. Wyatt Fisher, a licensed psychologist, marriage counsellor, and a niche dating site founder, "Becoming exclusive is a risk because both must be willing to put aside

all other possible relationships for one another." "Getting married is a massive risk, where both spouses are willing to permanently put aside all other relationships for one another." Whether commitment does or doesn't look like marriage for you and your partner, it's still a bit of a risk, but it will certainly require you to trust and respect one another, bringing you closer together.

6. Speaking Up
Speaking up when you disagree with your partner—especially if it's something that's really important to you—can be a good risk. It can be intimidating to vocally disagree with someone close to you, even if you think the relationship is rock-solid, but ultimately, it could help the two of you better understand each other.

7. Taking on A Joint Challenge
A physical or fitness challenge such as going on a bike trip, running a marathon, completing 20 workouts in 30 days, etc. allows you to encourage each other and there is some healthy competition—both lead to stronger connection. Plus, yes, you'll be competing a little bit, but you'll also feel like you're on the same team, working toward the same goal.

Furthermore, teamwork can definitely bring the two of you closer together and make your relationship that much stronger.

Recap: Seven (7) Risks Worth Taking:

1. Sharing Your Fantasies or Mixing Things Up a Bit
2. Moving
3. Going to Couples Therapy
4. Starting a Family
5. Committing
6. Speaking Up
7. Taking on A Joint Challenge

How to Build Trust in Your Relationship

1. Be true to your word and follow through with your actions

The point of building trust is for others to believe what you say. Keep in mind, however, that building trust requires not only keeping the promises you make, but also not making promises you're unable to keep.

Keeping your word shows others what you expect from them, and in turn, they'll be more likely to treat you with respect, developing further trust in the process.

2. Learn how to communicate effectively with others

Poor communication is a major reason why relationships break down. Good communication includes being clear about what you have or have not committed to and what has been agreed upon.

Building trust is not without risk. It involves allowing both you and others taking risks to prove trustworthiness. To navigate this, effecttive communication is key. Without it, you may find the messages you've intended to send aren't the messages that are received.

3. Remind yourself that it takes time to build and earn trust

Building trust is a daily commitment. Don't make the mistake of expecting too much too soon. In order to build trust, first take small steps and take on small commitments and then, as trust grows, you will be more at ease with making and accepting bigger commitments. Put trust in, and you will generally get trust in return.

4. Take time to make decisions and think before acting too quickly

Only make commitments that you are happy to agree to. Have the courage to say "no," even when it disappoints someone. If you agree to something and can't follow through, everyone involved is worse off.

Be clear about what you have on your plate, and keep track of your commitments. Being organized is a necessary part of building trust with family, friends and colleagues. It enables you to make a clear decision as to whether to agree to requests of your time and energy.

5. Value the relationships that you have—and don't take them for granted

Trust often results from consistency. We tend to have the most trust in people who are there for us consistently through good times and bad. Regularly showing someone that you're there for them is an effective way to build trust.

6. Develop your team skills and participate openly

When you take an active role in a team and make contributions, people are more likely to respect and trust you. It's also imperative when building trust in a team to show your willingness to trust others.

Being open and willing to make contributions and to engage demonstrates this. In other words, take what others say into consideration, show that you are listening actively, suggest your thoughts and feedback in a respectful way and demonstrate that you are willing to be part of the team.

7. Always be honest

The message you convey should always, always be the truth. If you are caught telling a lie, no matter how small, your trustworthiness will be diminished.

8. Help people whenever you can

Helping another person, even if it provides no benefit to you, builds trust. Authentic kindness helps to build trust.

9. Don't hide your feelings

Being open about your emotions is often an effective way to build trust. Furthermore, if people know that you care, they are more likely to trust you.

Emotional intelligence plays a role in building trust. Acknowledging your feelings, learning the lessons that prevail and taking productive action means that you won't deny reality—this is the key to building trust.

10. Don't always self-promote

Acknowledgment and appreciation play an important role in building trust and maintaining good relationships. Recognizing and appreciaeciating the efforts of others shows your talented for leadership and teamwork and increases the trust others have in you.

On the other hand, if people don't demonstrate appreciation for a good deed, they appear selfish. Selfishness destroys trust.

11. Always do what you believe to be right

Doing something purely for approval means sacrificing your own values and beliefs. This decreases trust in yourself, your values and your beliefs. Always doing what you believe is right, even when others disagree, will lead others to respect your honesty.

Interestingly, when building trust, you must be willing to upset others on occasion. People tend not to trust those who simply say whatever they think others want to hear.

12. Admit your mistakes

When you attempt to hide your mistakes, people know that you are being dishonest. By being open, you show your vulnerable side, and this helps build trust with other people.

This is because they perceive you to be more like them—everyone makes mistakes. If you pretend that you never make mistakes, you'll make it difficult for others to trust you because you have created an unnecessary difference between the two of you. When all that a person sees is the "perfection" you project, they likely won't trust you.

Recap: Twelve (12) Ways to Build Trust In Your Relationship:

1. Be True to Your Word and Follow Through with Your Actions
2. Learn How to Communicate Effectively with Others
3. Remind Yourself That It Takes Time to Build and Earn Trust
4. Take Time to Make Decisions and Think Before Acting Too Quickly
5. Value the Relationships that You Have – and Don't Take Them for Granted
6. Develop Your Team Skills and Participate Openly
7. Always Be Honest
8. Help People Whenever You Can
9. Don't Hide Your Feelings
10. Don't Always Self-Promote
11. Always Do What You Believe to be Right
12. Admit Your Mistakes

Partnering and Development

Trust is necessary for emotional intimacy and that is necessary for a healthy, close relationship. It's much easier and faster to lose trust than it is to build it up. To develop trust with your partner, you need to "say what you mean and mean what you say".

As young children, we quickly learn to tell if someone is being untruthful. It may be that someone doesn't follow through with their promises, or a parent makes threats they don't follow through on. This form of self-protection evolved to help us survive, so nearly all of us are able to notice the "proverbial boy crying wolf".

As we grow older, we finetune our expectations and behavior by learning not to trust an untruthful person, which helps protect ourselves from being let down again. So, when trying to develop trust in a relationship, don't say things that you won't follow through with.

It's also important not to say things that don't accurately reflect how you feel. Consistently telling lies, even if they feel small or inconsequential, will result in the other person no longer trusting what you say.

Another aspect of building trust is to become increasingly vulnerable in the relationship as it develops. People feel trust when they rely on one another. In the relationships we have, we build trust through vulnerability. Part of this will happen automatically over time through our daily interactions—such as feeling assured that our partner will be there if they have offered to pick us up from work.

It is also important to be emotionally vulnerable. Building trust requires you to open yourself up to the potential risk of being hurt. This could be revealing things that scare you or exposing aspects of yourself that you don't consider attractive. In other words, trust is developed when our partners have the chance to let us down or hurt us, but they don't.

Respect plays an important role in trust. One of the most emotionally enduring ways we can be harmed by our partners is if they belittle us or look at us with condescension or contempt, because a lack of respect destroys trust.

Any relationship, even that between a sales assistant and customer, involves a basic level of trust, and thus respect. However, maintaining that basic level of respect becomes even more important the more emotionally intimate the relationship is.

Unfortunately, we occasionally show our partners our worst qualities. We may be more prone to lash out at people we are close to than we would at a stranger. We lose sight of the fact that respect is even more significant to those we love due to the harm that lack of respect over time will cause.

It's not necessary to be perfectly polite all the time with your partner. However, remember that every time you treat your partner in a way that breaches a basic level of respect, you will damage the connection you have. Plus, it will make it more challenging for your partner to trust you over time.

Additionally, to build trust with your partner, be prepared to give him or her the benefit of the doubt. For this idea, Bonior gives the example of a patient and his doctor, who he's been seeing for ten years and who he trusts and respects.

Bonior describes the difference between how the patient feels about the trusted doctor's opinion and the opinion of a doctor whom the patient has never seen before. While the patient may be prepared to have confidence in the new doctor because of her medical qualifications, it is likely that he will feel a lot more comfortable with the doctor with whom he has developed trust.

It may even be easier for him to hear difficult or surprising medical news from his regular doctor because he will be prepared to give the doctor the benefit of the doubt because of the trust and history they share.

One more way to build trust in a relationship is to express your feelings in a functional, helpful way. An important component of emotional intimacy is being able to talk about one's feelings without shouting, verbally attacking or shutting down the conversation.

Therefore, in order to build trust, develop ways to discuss difficult feelings that are collaborative and respectful. To build trust, you need to give your partnerthe chance to connect with the "real" you—which includes your emotional complexity (Bonior, 2018).

Finally, to build trust with your partner in a marriage or relationship, it is important to consider reciprocity (Bonior, 2018). In other words, be willing to give as well as receive. It is necessary for both partners to feel comfortable with the levels of giving and receiving.

Do things together that benefit others

One the most powerful ways of staying close and connected is to jointly focus on something you and your partner value outside of the relationship. Volunteering for a cause, project or community work that has meaning for both of you can keep a relationship fresh and interesting. It can also expose you both to new people and ideas, offer the chance to tackle new challenges together and provide fresh ways of interacting with each other.

Additionally, this helps to relieve stress, anxiety and depression; doing things to benefit others delivers immense pleasure. Human beings are hard-wired to help others. The more you help, the happier you'll feel as individuals and as a couple.

Good communication is a fundamental part of a healthy relationship. When you experience a positive emotional connection with your partner, you feel safe and happy. When people stop communicating well, they stop relating well, and times of change or stress can really bring out the disconnect. It may sound simplistic, but as long as you are communicating, you can usually work through whatever problems you're facing.

Take In Love to Hedge Your Bets

Writers from the Gestalt school of therapy describe what they call a person's growing edge. They imagine that each person is a little like an expanding circular galaxy. Deep inside, at the center of the galaxy, is your comfort zone. This area is very familiar to you. It feels safe. This is where you keep all the habits of a lifetime. We have little anxiety within this zone because it is safe.

Way outside the comfort zone is the area of the complete unknown. You might say that this is like the astronomer's idea of "dark matter." There's something out there all right, something completely unknown and impossible to describe. The complete unknown fills people with vague feelings of dread: "I don't know what's out there, and I'm not sure I want to find out." The most interesting part of a person's life is at the growing edge.

Metaphorically, this area is at the edge of your personal comfort zone, in the narrow space between the safe and the unsafe, the familiar and the unfamiliar, the known and the unknown. People feel excited when they reach their growing edge because they sense that here is where they can expand their sense of being. The growing edge is a little scary because you are venturing into new territory. Nevertheless, it's not terrifying because it's been within sight for a while.

Here's an example. Sheila grew up in a big city; however, she's always been drawn toward the outdoors. Once, several years ago, she considered just chucking her city life, buying a farm and winging it, but she didn't follow through right then because she figured she'd fail at farming. Sheila was right at that time. She didn't know enough to succeed. She signed up for some horticulture classes at the local university, took a master gardening class and began raising cash crops on a small plot of land she rented from a nearby farmer. Sheila eventually became skillful. Then the farmer decided to retire. Sheila took a deep breath and bought his land. She still doesn't know if she will succeed, but she feels well enough prepared to take the chance. She's at her growing edge in life, the place between the known and the unknown.

You probably have growing edges in every major area of your life. Take work as an example. Certainly, there are aspects of your job you can almost do in your sleep. These are tasks within your comfort zone. Then there are other things you could never hope to do at all because they are in your unknown area, but finally there are duties you are just now beginning to tackle. You haven't mastered them yet so they take a lot of thought and energy. These new challenges exist at your growing edge. They may raise your anxiety a bit, but without these new challenges work would even- tually become pretty boring.

Taking in love presents challenges for just about everybody. That means there are occa- sions and circumstances in which taking in your partner's love comes easily and naturally (when you are within your comfort zone), then there are probably times when you cannot imagine taking in love (maybe when your partner is angry with you or when you are very busy with something else). These situations exist in your unknown area. Moreover, there are your growing edge opportunities—situations in which you are just learning how to take in your partner's love and care.

Human beings have a natural reaction to pain: they want to avoid it as much as possible. That simple desire protects us from suffering need-lessly and sometimes keeps us alive. Unfor-tunately, though, it's possible to get too good at avoiding potentially painful situations espec-ially in the area of taking in another's love.

Here's what happens.

You fall in love with someone
Who promises to always love,
Cherish and respect you.

However,
they instead hurt and even betray you.
So you end that relationship
emotionally damaged.
Maybe it happens again.

If so, maybe that's when you decide to stay distant. "*I'm no fool,*" you say to yourself. "Why should I open myself up to more heartache by loving and trusting someone new? Look what's happened to me already. I'm better off shutting down my need for others. True, I'm a little lonely now, but at least I'm safe. I'll never let anyone break my heart again." You stop trusting others, even the people who say they love you.

Although we're describing adult love relationships here, it is possible that you began shutting out others much earlier in life. Maybe in childhood you made a decision to stay safe by not letting people get close to you. That sometimes happens when parents are unreliable or dangerous, when someone you loved a lot died, or sometimes just because members of your family weren't very good at expressing love and so you quit, hoping for it. Perhaps you've never recovered from when your first real love fell apart in your teens. Sure, others tell you to get over that lost love and get on with life, but it's not that easy. Whenever the disaster struck, whether you were ten years old, twenty or forty, it had a devastating effect. It made you scared to fall in love again. Ever since then, you've played life safer, like an investor hedging his or her bets to be sure not to lose rather than playing to win.

We want to suggest, strongly, that it's time to accept the pain from your past by letting it stay in the past. Yes, you've been hurt, badly, but it's over. You survived. You've learned enough from whatever happened to protect yourself better. You've also probably learned one of life's most bittersweet truths: bad things can happen to you no matter how good and decent a person you are. We're not suggesting that you set yourself up for abuse or betrayal. No. You have every right to protect yourself. But isn't it time, now, for you to start letting in love from those people who have earned your trust? There's no sense waiting for some guarantee that you'll never be hurt again because life never offers such certainties.

Love And Trust Form a Strong Bond

"I love you. You can trust me."

It isn't always easy to trust another human being. Trust involves vulnerability, and being vulnerable means you could get hurt. Just because you love your partner or your partner loves you doesn't necessarily mean that you trust each other. It's certainly possible to love without trust. However, usually relationships are based only on love; therefore, those in which trust is absent, are unstable. They break down easily in the midst of lies, omissions and irresponsibility. However, coupling love with trust is like supergluing two people together. The bond created when love is mixed with trust becomes almost unbreakable. One difference between love and superglue, though, is that developing trust is a slow process, made even slower if your partner has been betrayed in the past. That's why it's so important for you to be consistently trustworthy.

Just saying "I love you" is not enough. You must show your love as well if you want your partner to feel loved. That idea goes for both parties in matters of trust. You can't expect your partner to trust you unless you act in a trustworthy manner.

What does it mean to be trustworthy? Here are five traits of a trustworthy person.

1. He or she says the truth, especially in important conversations with his or her partner.
2. He or she doesn't omit important things from conversations, even when mentioning them might be embarrassing or troubling.
3. He or she keeps promises, not only big ones (like a vow to be sexually faithful) but also little day-to-day agreements.
4. He or she behaves responsibly, reliably and consistently when it comes to executing daily routines that he or she can be dependable.
5. He or she admits when he or she has screwed up and makes amends.

The challenge is to do all five of these things all of the time. Perhaps, being merely human, that is asking too much. We all fail the test of trustworthiness once in a while. However, if you want to build trust in your relationship, you should strive to be completely trustworthy, not to be mostly trustworthy or trustworthy when it's convenient. One warning: although being honest is an important part of building trust, remember that you can be tactful and honest at the same time. You won't build trust through honesty if you pair honesty with cruelty, tactle-ssness, crudeness or thoughtlessness.

Take The Leap

Even now, if you feel some apprehension or are unable to trust your partner, the road ahead will be hard, but you are not without hope. Every day we are given opportunities to build our trust and mature in our resolve. It might be the smallest act, but something in your ability to deliver on a promise conveys to your spouse a larger narrative. We all want to feel like we have someone to depend on. Failure to be trustworthy causes so many issues in life. When people say, "It's the little things", those small little life lessons are what they are referring to. Taking out the trash when agreed to, wearing that lingerie col-lecting dust spontaneously and doubling down on caring for your spouse are all ways to solidify their ability to trust you. If you can harness the moments life gives you to cement your love, go for it.

Personally, one of the earliest moments like that for us, was when a few months into our relationship, my car was totaled. Micah was the first person I called to talk through it with. He came to help me sort through the rubble and move forward. I was safe and physically unharmed, but rather emotional. It was something small in the grand scheme of things, but it made me feel safe, protected and cared for when he was there. In an unexpressed and later realized way, those were the qualities I was seeking in a partner. That is what I saw in my grandparents' marriage and wanted for myself. I needed someone who would have my back and I could reciprocate, but it would be difficult to get there without trust. You have to buy into that person and take stock in what they say they feel about you.

Trusting someone is a big step for the average person. It's me. I'm the average person. Opening up my life, my heart and my wallet in total partnership with someone was a big ask; and in our case, the "not asking" is kind of what led us to this idea of total togetherness. It was organic for us. I think we both kind of decided early on to let it (our relationship) do whatever it was gonna do and just be open to the outcome. The no pressure thing was what really sealed the deal. We were honest and communicated at a very intimate level, so neither of us had to ask "what is this?" or "what are we doing?" I mean, we did ask after the fact, but only out of habit. Honestly, it just felt right. It still does. More than 10 years and 100 other calculated risks later, here we are, still together. Imagine the best thing ever and that's it. It's not willy-nilly or whimsical. They don't call it a calculated risk for nothing. Love is a trust fall, but one that should be approached with a mixture of reckless abandon and planned forethought. At the end of the day, that is the endgame: Togetherness.

www.ingramcontent.com/pod-product-compliance
Lightning Source LLC
Chambersburg PA
CBHW060240030426
42335CB00014B/1540